T0368333

CORONA CRISIS CHRONICLES

Three Cs in a Row

R E J W A N A L I

authorHOUSE

AuthorHouse™
1663 Liberty Drive
Bloomington, IN 47403
www.authorhouse.com
Phone: 1 (833) 262-8899

Because of the dynamic nature of the Internet, any web addresses or links contained in this book may have changed since publication and may no longer be valid. The views expressed in this work are solely those of the author and do not necessarily reflect the views of the publisher, and the publisher hereby disclaims any responsibility for them.

Any people depicted in stock imagery provided by Getty Images are models, and such images are being used for illustrative purposes only.
Certain stock imagery © Getty Images.

This book is printed on acid-free paper.

ISBN: 978-1-6655-0372-3 (sc)
978-1-6655-0371-6 (e)

Print information available on the last page.

Published by AuthorHouse 10/19/2020

authorHOUSE®

TABLE OF CONTENTS

Author's note:

*I was planning to pull curtain after ten writings for this title. However, additional three just came in that stream that I could not help but to add on!

EPISODE # 1

"What Do You Care What Other People Think?"

My dad, who is now in his eighties, had three master's degrees during the Pakistan Era, Dacca University (Supervisor: Bose Professor Abdul Matin Chowdhury), American University of Beirut (Lebanon), and University of New South Wales (Australia) but never could win a PhD. For obvious reasons he used to despise PhDs. His persistent logic has been PhD makes people arrogant and often takes away the bare minimum capacity to think/talk scientifically/rationally. The PhDs have lost the capacity to listen to other people's views. When in a room, you have too many of them it's total chaos! Interestingly in Rajshahi University (RU) campus lot of PhD-less people used to have similar views as they used to call PhDs "PiazDee" that means discussion over onions . . . shading off tears over nonsense . . . leading nowhere.

Sometimes you can call it hunting deer (Dr) so that you can have fiesta—not a vegetarian peaceful option as most good things can be done in more peaceful and harmonious ways. So what could be the definition of PhDs? Some says "Permanent Head Damages." Well, there is some truth there as we all agree . . . But then, why does that happen? What are the possible causes/reasons behind? I guess the answer could be "Painful Hopeless Days." People spending six years plus time in that process can develop lot of bad symptoms. In contrast, smart/lucky people with shortened period in that process can call it "Perfect Happy Days" . . . Interestingly, both processes turn out to give people common shape "Talk More, Listen Less" . . . Maybe in Feynman's great words: "What Do You Care What Other People Think?"

Journals of New York City, May 31, 2020
Oakland Gardens, New York

Artificial Intelligence, Machine Languages and Homeopathy

So here goes the story. A friend of mine from post-doc days, after a few years of no-communication, shoot me an e-mail that he would be coming to New York City for a conference. He was then in the US West Coast area doing research in an academic/industry institution in a senior capacity. After couple of emails, we talked over the phone and he mentioned the paper he would present was on the topics of big data analysis, machine languages, and artificial intelligences. This was about six or seven years back as everyone is now feeling omnipresent media pressure from Artificial Intelligence and Machine Languages; but a few years back that was not the scenario.

I have never liked Starbucks coffee chain that much due to its bitter taste, but my friend made a concession here as you know well in American intelligentsia Starbucks is in an upper tier like Mac over Windows. If someone takes average education of customers drinking coffee from Starbucks to Dunkin Donuts, Starbucks will score higher here for sure. So I felt good as my friend agreed to spend time to have coffee in the Dunkin Donut shop after his key days in the meeting.

My friend had all the excitement as he was telling how many of his colleagues/collaborators from past days applauded his works. Some Ivy League professors were also in the room and did pay heavy tributes to his science. I was listening as well as counting faces of cops of Bangladesh origin in New York Police Department (NYPD) uniform. Many places in New York City you will find very professional cop teams comprised of men and women entirely of Bangladesh origin. Some sociologists can make comparative studies of similar people in Bangladesh Police uniform versus NYPD uniform. When our daughter was around five and used to be in a stroller with us, we used to roam around all over New York City for museums, historical places, restaurants, never did these hearty gentle professional folks let us carry her over long vertical stairs. By the way, most subway stations in New York City do not have decent elevators in contrast to many subway systems in the world.

"What do you think of artificial intelligence?" I was pulled back from my reverie and right into a trail of his speech. "They are the same like homeopathy." My answer was bit off-the-guard and flat. My friend was flabbergasted. He started to have serious allergic reactions as he was coughing and gasping. I hastened to find a glass of cold water for him. He started to breathe normal gradually, with occasional heavy sighs and could not believe on what ground our friendship has been standing on so far. The reaction was not fake and truly genuine; just suppleness of his tender love for AI so shaken by some very obtuse remarks here that later he said he never expected from me in the first place. Realizing an unexpected cloud looming over our friendship, I started trying to ameliorate the situation. I was telling him a positive story from a magazine how a person was trying hotwiring his stalled car in FDR with bottle of water from East River after losing the original car keys in upstate Hudson River using the Principle of Homeopathy. But it was even deteriorating the scenario more and more. I was cursing myself and deciding not to carry such asperity in opinion next time I talked to people talking about new things in the world. Against the principle of "Talk More, Listen Less", I decided to listen to him.

"You know what, you have no idea what you're talking about. You never read a book on AI/ML. Perhaps never you took any course on AI in graduate school, and that's why you're saying so," my friend resumed his speech in a more controlled manner as I nodded gently. Seeing an apparent attentive listener, my friend quickly got back into his enthusiasm in full. Now he started telling me how chips plugged in and around the head will start to read a professor's mind and start sending information to GPUs in massive parallel to accelerate publications and patent applications. All the research impact factors will be displayed in dazzling billboards with special effects in Times Square or Piccadilly Circus as outreach efforts in science. There will even be back-up hardware in case original chips plugged round the professor's skull get disconnected to keep a seamless flow of information in science. I started to like and love my friend as he had been really working hard on exonerating the academic folks from the burden of publishing to avoid perishing. In New York City, crowded coffee shops are not an ideal place to hang out like forever before the pandemic days, of course. After checking out from Dunkin Donuts, we decided to take a walk toward Central Park block. My friend offered me a cigarette from his packet of Marlboro, but I declined gently as I already quit what used to be an essential ingredient in my solitary homework problem-solving sessions, way back in graduate school days.

Journals of New York City || June 03, 2020
Oakland Gardens, New York

EPISODE # 3

Curfews and New York City

This week New York City had a few curfews. In the history of Bangladesh, the term "curfews" has quite a big importance. A significant percentage of Bangladesh history can be elaborated by the intricacies of curfews—from a group of people imposing curfews over the groups of people trying to violate or break free from the curfews. From August 14, 1947 to December 16, 1971, one can chronologically record how many curfews had been implemented by ruling groups and violated—or at least attempted to violate—by other groups of people. In post-liberation era, a lot of state honors and recognitions have been awarded to people living or posthumously, associated with breaking of curfews during the Pakistan Era. You can say in terms of so-called Marxism-Leninism, bourgeois is usually the class trying to impose curfews over the working class. So the elite or the bourgeois will design curfews fortified with state-funded machineries. On the other hand, working class, while trying to bring about changes, will try to break the curfews by their sheer political zeal with or without venture funding. Interestingly, two megacities in the world, Hong Kong and New York City, are now going through turbulent times, and each controlling group is making claims of auspicious, generous hidden foreign funding working actively behind. People with experience in Bangladesh student politics can tell how difficult it is to keep the critical mass needed for movements with activists without adequate supplies of tea, samosas, and high quality cigarettes, even though you have a sound agenda with good moral and political reasons. Anyway, through all these, can you foresee the dangers of a world militantly dominated by non-English-speaking people in the first place? The British taught us at least the right language to learn and earn your bread with some reasonable dignity all over the globe. If both New York City and Hong Kong crumble, we will then only have London, Toronto, and maybe Sydney. Only my personal hope and solution here, with my wife Sayma being fluent in Hindi and Urdu migration to Bombay or Dubai or maybe to Karachi or Lahore, might be options, kind of a repatriation solution for the nationals of then-defunct East Pakistan in early 1970s in BD's post-liberation period, not a glorified choice or path in 2020, of course.

Going back to the subject of curfew, the very first one I can still vividly remember was on August 15, 1975. The post-liberation period in mid-1970s was quite a difficult time for the Bangladesh's middle class compared to the conveniences of East Pakistan Era in the 1960s. I was not even born yet in the 1960s but I had been heavily indoctrinated in the ideas at least; and many here probably may or may not agree with that. Along with some strange collections of research grade wools called Merino and non-Merino types that dad brought from Australia, a West German-made typewriter that he used to type his research papers of brand "abc 2000," mom-owned "Singer" sewing machine, we used to have a valve-operated "PYE" radio besides some basic furniture in our Science Lab quarter. When I visited Amish County in Pennsylvania a few years back, I realized they had a lot better amenities than we used to have in Science Lab campus during that period.

In the morning of August 15, 1975, we heard some husky voices of military officers coming via radio broadcast from the PYE set with loud background noise as the radio set needed to be connected to 220 volt power supply to keep the thermionic valves running compared to today's solar/free energy electronics about the coup d'état that happened in the early hour of August 15, 1975. He was warning each Bangladesh national (then Bengali) of extreme and severe outcome should someone dare to break the curfews. For us, that meant "no schools." I just started in the Experimental School in Rajshahi University Campus early that year. With very few families residing inside Science Lab campus, we had the advantages of isolation from the political turbulences in the '70s through the '90s. Never a single person died from political violence inside the campus, not even one got seriously hurt or injured through fist-fighting due to politically polarized opinions, whereas it was not that uncommon among educated classes in post-liberation Bangladesh. I guess Dhaka and Chittagong Science Lab campuses might have similar unique records. So the thumb rule for us in the campus to stay safe had been if you did not show up ostensibly near the two main gates opposite of Rajshahi University campus, you were fine from the army, BDR, Rakkhi Bahini, and their minimal heckling of getting your hair badly cropped, bald or unwanted tattoos all over your body. Luckily, RAB did not exist in those days.

Incidentally, in that August period, we had two of our aunts visiting us from Bogra town. "Indian Army will invade us soon. I only wish they take over. These people are traitors," one of my aunts commented during a tense and gloomy late lunch on that fateful August 15. The other aunt said, "It will be Confederation with

Pakistan as per six-point formula." In other words, it seemed that the existence of Independent Bangladesh was under serious jeopardy after the assassination of the president; it was swinging either to India's or Pakistan's way. The cloud of uncertainty did not change much later on. That evening, one of my two aunts was crying and sobbing in contrast to the prevailing emotion in our house. "You just killed your father, you traitor. Who trained you to operate sten guns? You all will be tried in this very soil." Three sons of my aunt fought against Pakistani forces in the battlefields face-to-face; this was in contrast to our family. In Bogra town, her house heavily fired, subjected to arson and each of them was chased down for their lives while many of us were just complying with the curfews rather than break it. Although reluctant to participate in the rapid process of harvesting fortune of independence via plundering process in 1972–75 period, her entire family did carry lifetime commitments to just slain first president of Bangladesh like they had for Indira Gandhi. However, that evening, my aunt seemed to be alone in her sole and strange opinion on the killings of the president as the fate of his family members were not known that time yet. Looking back from the course of the history of Bangladesh over the years, I learned a lesson even though I was just a kid on August 15, 1975: "Opinion should not be subjugated, must be sympathetically listened, and if possible, should be time stamped."

Journals of New York City || June 05, 2020
Oakland Gardens, New York

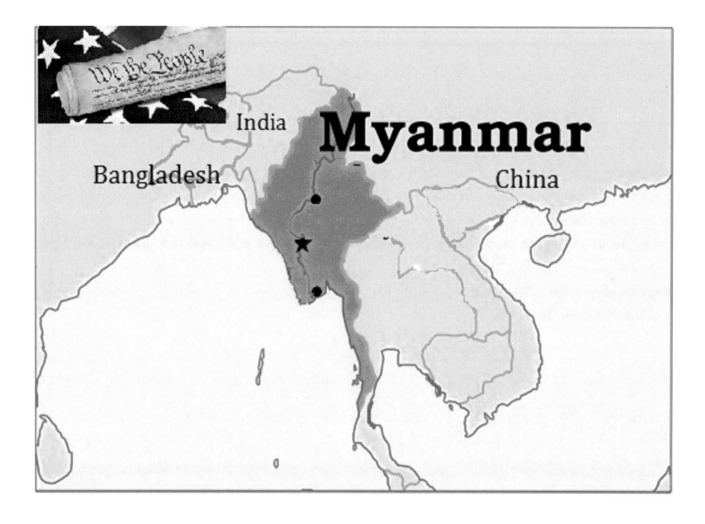

EPISODE # 04

Zulfi Is My Friend and the US Constitution

This year US presidential election means more politics and debates. In the last four years, US has been experiencing undermining and corrosion of its democratic institutions. Still now, US can rightfully claim it has the best-written Constitution on earth, even over many European countries with longer democratic heritages. When you are born in a culture or religion, you don't need to study the main scripture or the book of your culture because by birth you belong there. But if you want to be bit exploratory and even thinking of conversion/transformation not via coercion rather by perception, you probably will shop around in the bookstore or try online to read among the scriptures, compare, and then choose. In today's world, coercion hardly happens much like in the past, but things like jobs, social benefits, and marriages can a lot of times play catalytic factors in actuating cultural/religious transformations. In that case, cultural/religious leaders often with little nominal or no-fee bypass the "Basic Scripture Test Kits" and embrace the new-coming member with a big hug and smile along with applause from communities. Unfortunately, the US naturalization system is not that so auspicious and welcoming. You have to convince federal officers via several stages in interviews that you have a reasonable understanding of the US Constitution, culture, and history; and have to pass a reasonable standard test. So like transformed persons by perception, US-naturalized citizens have advantages over citizens by birth in terms of fundamental understandings of the US Constitution, unless they decide to have a copy themselves and spend time to self-educate, reading from cover to cover. Often, political adversaries say our current president has been suffering from the above limitations concerning his knowledge of the US Constitution.

Shifting from the US scenario, let us do a Thought (Gedanken) experiment with Rohynga issue that currently Bangladesh has been experiencing in the last few years. We will translate things a little backward in time axis, which physicists often can do if not in real world but in paper and pencil at least. Think of the

Rohynga scenario just after post-liberation period in Bangladesh in the 1970s. As we all know, China did not support our Liberation War in 1971. So it is quite judicious to visualize a picture soon after the Liberation War with Bhutto (Zulfi), who had always been a sinister master planner, planning to give Mujib hard times and make influential presence in that region; Chow-En-Lie asked Burma to push Rohyngas into Bangladesh border to undermine Mujib and his administration, who had been already preoccupied with a lot of domestic problems in post-liberation period. Bhasani was in a confused state as ever like Imran Khan is now, and was undecided if to criticize or not the crisis of the Sino–Burmese move. Ultra-left lobby in NAP said he should not criticize as through these Sino–Burmese actions prospects were there for an immensely beneficial and still cheap like 99c "Made in China Red Revolution" in the long run. Other groups said he should immediately demand Mujib to take steps and go for hunger strike. After the removal of India's Army, Mujib had bit of a cold relationship with Indira as Indira had been undecided and was watchful of the situation for some time and not committing anything as per the twenty-five-year Indo–Bangladesh pacts.

So it was a tough situation for the president. So Mujib decided to summon Shafiullah, Zia, A. K. Khondoker, M. H. Khan, Khaled Mosharraf, and even Colonel Taher, Qadir Siddique to his office in BongoBhaban to discuss the crisis. Dr. Kamal was also present in the meeting as the foreign minister. In the international scenario despite Bhutto's intriguing roles, OIC and Arab League had already started to criticize Sino-backed Burmese moves. Brezhnev had been consistently in touch with Indira and appeared like he would ask Soviet representatives to discuss the issues in UNO's Security Council because he had been suspicious with the situation getting outside of Soviet influence and also had pressure from within Warsaw Pacts nations. Kissinger had been quite perplexed and taken by *shock and awe* by these Sino–Burmese moves and had been advising Nixon ever since to keep the Seventh Fleet ready if situation worsened and to keep a strong presence in the belt in case Red Revolution engulfed the region beyond predicted course. Under such global situation, the following conversations were going on in Dacca in BongoBhavan:

President Mujib: "Shafiullah, what do you think we should do now? You know the developments in the southeast border, right?"

Shafiullah: "Sir, sir, we will put a lot of forces around Dhamondi 32 and will make sure in the worst case that you and your family can cross the border to India. I will make sure all leading Awami League leaders in the government can also cross the border safely like they did in 1971 because situation seems very risky."

President Mujib was very annoyed and looking at Zia and Khaled Musharraf who had already started murmuring if they had any better things to say here. Zia seemed composed and told Mujib the following:

Zia: "Sir, we are in a lot better situation than a couple years back in 1971. All we need to mobilize the tank and artillery divisions with air support. We can push back Burmese forces deep inside the Rakhaine state control line. In the meantime, we need to train Rohyngas in a similar model India did for us in 1971. But we can rein control until they are ready to take over Rakhaine state under UN/International Forces. In the meantime, please request Indira at least to be neutral here and stop any military supplies if they have any through open or secret deals to Burmese authority. Also tell your friends in *Tripura and West Bengal and all over India* to put pressure on Shrimati so that at least she criticizes the refugee crisis like she did in 1971." Khaled, Khondoker, M. H. Khan were nodding and seemed like Zia's idea but Taher seemed not happy and was grudging little bit and was saying, "Maolana Bhasani may not like it."

President Mujib was a bit irritated with Taher. "Do not talk for others. Say if you support Zia's idea or not, I know Maolana well than you know him," but started to laugh soon, looking at Zia. "All the time you try to do things your way bypassing me. I tell you all are witnesses here, Khaled, Shafiullah, Khondoker and Khan; I give Red Note here. Please look after Zia so that he cannot do things on his own like Jacob did bypassing Indira in 1971. I need to make a phone call to Kremlin and also need to talk to my friends in Eastern Europe. Opinion of UK's Edward Heath will also be important here as he can put the refugee crisis issues in Commonwealth Forum. We cannot feed them forever but we have moral obligations here as well."

"But also keep the forces ready if Burmese government does not behave, we may have to use that. I will request Asad and Sadat for four squadrons of Mig-21s and if possible some Mig-23s. Khondoker, talk with Bashar and select some good people from the air force for training as we may need to send them to Moscow or East Germany ASAP. Indira might be a bit uncomfortable but I will talk to her. I know Bhutto is playing games behind all these. You all know him, but still, he is my good personal friend, but in politics he always tries to show his skills even over Indira." Mujib's laugh was just spreading.

"None comes any closer to you even though both are from Oxford, I know you all three and I did also attend Oxford myself." Dr. Kamal seemed snapped into the conversations.

"I was a bit lucky to work closely with Sher-e-Bangla, Surawardhy, and Bhasani. You know after all, I was not born with a golden spoon to attend Oxford or Harvard like Kamal here," said the president in a self-effacing tone. "Also you don't need to do much yourself if Bhutto is around in the scene, and Yahya Khan and Tikkah Khan are also there."

"I know what you meant." Dr. Kamal started to laugh loudly as the rest of the people joined the laughter as well.

Journals of New York City || June 7, 2020
Oakland Gardens, New York

Corona Social Culture: Science Classes, Gun Control

Countries in the Asian subcontinent have strong family values and tradition of social bondages among kiths and kins in comparison to Western societies. Duties to parents are not just confined to sending greeting cards to mom or dad on fixed days in the year or merely visiting parents in old homes during holiday breaks as part of agenda toward the end of list. In some ways, the COVID-19 crisis has exposed in very painful ways some inherent flaws in the Western family structure. As you may remember during peak of the COVID-19 pandemic in New York City, almost all the old homes were totally forsaken by attending working groups and nurses for fear of being infected by the virus. These people, otherwise were supposed to take care of the elderly through any situation. If all those senior people had adequate individual family support in home settings, probably casualties would have been lot less. However, that might be just one side of the story. One may guess years back in their own time maybe that suffering senior population likely to be involved in evicting out their own sons or daughters out of their living places as they reach the age of eighteen. The bottom line is, without having domestic violations, Western societies have serious flaws of negligence to elder and aged populations and also carelessness to younger generations—and all are happening under strict federal and state laws and regulations. Probably that kind of extreme reality shape young people in different ways when they come to campuses for their college degrees in contrast to students in Bangladesh. They don't spare instructors usually older than their ages in the classrooms. The instructor has to defend his or her capacities and none can come in his or her defenses here.

In contrast to the above scenario, and looking back into Bangladesh's public universities, in most cases, if a student asks questions in a science class or tries seeking help with experiments in the lab, inevitably they will face negative reactions from the instructor. The instructor will immediately take it as a personal affront challenging his "unquestionable intellectual status" and will immediately think the student is ignoring his bulky PhD thesis or asking a tantalizingly designed questions to deliberately embarrass him or her in front of the class. Instead of encouraging or welcoming questions, the instructor with the privilege of speech will start to scorch the student with questions not relevant to that particular topic. The instructor will eventually lead and create such a situation in the class that student will start seeking apologies from the instructor, looking helplessly around at the classmates who had been already started grinning in rapport with the instructor's venerable opinion as all gazes are now directed to the student's follies, now exposed due to the very blunder of asking questions to an unquestionable person in the first place. The instructor would inevitably utilize the situation over the class in a way that next time onward during the entire stay of the student in the campus, they can never ask any more questions so as not to be ridiculed. Often instructors with noble hearts will avoid such public embarrassments of his/her students rather s/he would bring the student from the class to his/her office and would intellectually downsize/indoctrinate the student enough to make sure the student's academic curiosity is aligned with the instructor's publications/papers and glorious thinking patterns. Like exceptions above do not apply to all my great RU teacher friends particularly in Facebook who are in fact doing as good as anyone else and anywhere in the world and are not involved in creating above bitter experience for the young people and over their minds at all! Also, in my lucky years in Applied Physics and Electronics Department of RU, we used to have very capable world-class teachers who always did welcome questions in the classes and labs. Also, all the teachers used to encourage critical questionings and had been very helpful with lab experiments and debugging computer programs as well. Nowadays, sometimes I feel so sad and isolated that such a beautiful department can be obliterated from the map of RU campus. It is the same feeling of people without a state, or like refugees of a currently defunct state/country. Do you feel the same pain?

    After describing the reality of eviction of young people from their homes and habitats in the Western society, I started to feel and carry a deep sense guilt over the years while living in the USA for varied reasons. While most of my school and college friends after HSC had spread all over the world and immediately had started making marks in all frontier academic campuses with their talents and merits, I was still in RU campus often having delicious curries with obtuse insensibility to global intellect growth around. Rather, I had confined interests in cooked Hilsha from Rajshahi's Padma, samosas of Sahib Bazar or biryani of Pritom also from Sahib Bazar. My pocket money was enough for 7 to 10 sticks of Benson & Hedges or 555 (Bangla five) brand cigarettes as component of domestic meal plan and still I had been enrolled in university and was expecting and working on my BS (?) degree.

Getting back to campus violence issue here, in those days in RU premises the student violence frequencies were like traffic tickets in New York City—very common feature, recurring and persistent. Sometimes those RU student political campus closures used to last for almost one year or for several months. Now I feel besides counting COVID-19 deaths in Bangladesh, it would be a good idea to systematically study the origins of student violations in RU and other campuses, tally the number of casualties, identify the sources of original inspirations (Was it some continuation as per Great Mujib's March 7 speech or Major Zia's Kallurghat military declaration; or something more in line with the battles of Ohud or Badar?). I feel, however, that a *broader picture* of lay-people can be integrated into perception for greater social changes here that students' political wings and their patrons behind the curtains,, at different stages in their careers, have been tirelessly trying to achieve in Motihar (RU) campus. I know it is not sweet rather caustic and sometimes can really be bitter. But the way the student violence video from BUET did surface up (I guess in last year it was), and, hence, did indeed show and carry those legacies in close-knit and all well-related connected dots here. Interestingly, if you ask the older generation, they will boastfully say how peaceful they used to be in their own time compared to the present violent generation:

"We never used fire arms; only hockey sticks, cricket bats in solving issues and problems. All this violence is due to fire arms and not anything else." Given the gravity of present-day situations, we need to listen back to our elders' advice and must try not to waste lives either physical or intellectual through fruitless intellectual violence/turbulence and excursions. Let Young People Grow Their Ways and not under Your Shadow. You Better Stay in Your Own Shadow; in Your Well-Earned Comfort and Patron Umbrella but let Young People Grow and Bathe Their Ways Under the Bright Sun. Amen.

Disclaimer: The author has no conflicts of interest. Also there is absolutely no source of funding to declare unless you consider that *Time is Money.*

Journals of New York City || June 12, 2020
Oakland Gardens, New York

Reopening of New York City and the Sweet Mid-West

New York City (NYC) is gradually re-opening. Compared to many mid-West and South great cities like Chicago, Houston, Dallas, or maybe St. Louis, New York City has relatively few interstates crossing the city. Two relatively well-known such interstates and you may often find them in movies and literature are Brooklyn–Queens Expressway (BQE) and Long Island Expressway (LIE). Both are infamous for their clogged and congested traffics. When I moved to NYC in the fall of 2008, I instantly became a great fan of NYC drivers for several reasons. Given available road spaces for maneuvering your vehicles ratio-ed to the number of active vehicles, the number is way too low than most other cities. Considering that index number; traffic collisions are really very small compared to other cities, which shows NYC drivers are actually nationally better than anyone at least in terms of statistics. However, based on the collision safety index of the drivers, it is not advisable to build temptation to drive in NYC unless you have good reasons to do so. You will be way lot in better shape and in mental piece without a car and just using subways or public transports like many other cities in the world. You need to develop a different kind of driving sense even though you may be from San Francisco, Los Angeles, or Toronto. The only exception perhaps is if you have prior experience of driving in Dhaka; you're all set then and in fact you're overqualified but just need to make transition from Left to Right here.

When I came to the US almost twenty years ago in a nice beautiful mid-sized city called Wichita in Kansas, it took me quite time get over the psychological barrier that I would need to learn driving to survive in this country as rickshaws or public transportation did not exist anywhere; Uber like smartphone none probably could conceive that time. Like my US student visa, I was extremely fortunate to get a driver's license on my very first effort in less than three months from the date I arrived in the US, thank God. After my successful driving bid, I got a 1987 Mazda-626 for a mere $600 from an outgoing student. However, like any learning, driving has also many stages even with automatic transmission. You are a good skilled driver in changing lanes, stopping at signs, yielding to pedestrians—still you will have the initial trepidation when you first start to drive in the freeways. You need to manage your toy at an average 70 mph and need to get used to that frame of reference. Most of my friends in Wichita those days used to have that number at 90 mph. When I was driving in Colorado with two more friends with a rented car during a Fall break in one of my two-year stay in Kansas to make trip all around Denver, Boulder, Rocky Mountain National Parks, Colorado Springs, I realized I was still a novice in free-way driving compared to others with my driving skills with the jalopy of 1987 model Mazda-626.

"Bro, it is not TomTom* in your Rajshahi town. Can you please look at your rearview mirror and see how you're causing piling up traffic behind? Cheer up and speed up . . ." Radar was not that common those days also like the GPS, and we always need to look at road signs and exits relying on Rand McNally or AAA maps. I, in fact, was driving at 5 mph higher than the road sign limit of 70 mph. Both my friends' consensus of minimum required speed range seemed to be between 85 and 90 mph and could not compromise on my driving just at 10 mph less. The second friend said, "How did you escape Rajshahi and North Bengal in the first place with such low speed? You know in the world map it is one of the darkest places like black holes, I heard all from Rajshahi usually go to caverns in Afghanistan and get MS degree there." He just took a summer physics class and learned about escape velocity and black holes and quite excited about physics and even did come to me couple of times with freshman physics problems in the TA office but now paying me back for my dues in the office hours. ☺:) By the way, you all know after the tragedies of 9/11; referring to Afghanistan became quite a fashion to all ages of people. How they can so easily forget great Syed Mujtaba Ali** as so many of his great writings are based on just Kabul and Afghanistan! "You know what, I heard that you were actually ditched by a pretty girl originally from North Bengal in North–South campus and that's why you still cry in your sleep and even wet your bed sometimes." I was steadying the wheel as a trailer was

---

* TomTom is not a GPS brand here rather horse-driven cart similar like one can see in Central Park of New York City.

* An accomplished writer in Bengali literature and former faculty in Kabul University. Many of his famous writings were based in Afghanistan.

passing by us that moment and also looking at his reactions through rearview mirror, hoping it did not cause avalanche breakdown on him and overall inside the car. He seemed not to be bogged down at all via above although had been his Achilles' heels that transmitted by his roommate in Wichita who used to be with him in North-South University as well. Although bed-wetting obviously had been an exaggeration and retaliation here. ☺). "Thank God I was not stuck there. I have so many cheeky options now." He was laughing quite brazenly. "You fail in one case but seventy new options do open up. But for this life, you need to choose the leader of the seventy." All were laughing loudly after my improvisation.

Looking back in those days and particularly to the beauty of Colorado, I sometimes feel that perhaps I have already spent too long living in New York City. Mid-West also has its own beauty. Perhaps it may be the time to rediscover that again, who knows.

Disclaimer: PG-13 rated, discretion advised!

Journals of New York City: June 16, 2020
Oakland Gardens, New York

Rearview Mirror and Lane Changing

Despite heavily biased political views of civilian nature on undivided Pakistan, I started to fully utilize the freedom of reading and speech in post-BAKSAL era and started to develop a secret fondness for Bongobondhu, in line with two of my siblings and all the cousins. In national politics, it was President Zia's turn and public utterance of Bongobondhu that was almost condemned. Along with many colorful former Soviet-printed Bangla books from Mir or Progoti publishers with numerous titles inscribed with Lenin's mugshot as gifts from my political fugitive cousin, who had been crossing borders back and forth several times since August 15, 1975 as one of the wanted persons in Bogra town during President Zia's era, I got hold of a book titled *Ami Russel Bolchi* (আমি রাসেল বলছি) also from him. Forwarded by the spouse of Bose Professor Matin Chowdhury for whom dad had deep lifetime respect as his Master in Science (M.Sc.) supervisor in Dacca's Curzon Hall, the book had very mournful and tragic descriptions of the fate of slain President Mujib and his family members.

Anyway like my dad, I also had a renowned person as my M.Sc. supervisor in the now-defunct Applied Physics and Electronics Department in RU. Similar to Professor Matin Chowdhury, he also did become Vice-Chancellor of Rajshahi University. In fact, Professor S.R. Khan sir did surpass Dr. Matin Chowdhury in his achievements as he later also became ambassador of the People's Republic of Bangladesh to the United Kingdom, which Dr. Chowdhury never could make. Despite notoriety with some sections of people as "Caverns of Kabul/Kandahar in Bangladesh," RU campus in fact has often been oversighted for its nice teachings and research resources; perhaps good enough for a competent and sound undergrad science and research training. Honestly, I myself do feel "Caverns of Kandahar/Kabul of Bangladesh" is a bit of an exaggeration here as in reality, there used to be no such natural bunkers to hide in RU campus as in 1971, when the Indian Air Force started to pound heavily all over East Pakistan on the strongholds of Pakistan Forces positions everything actually fell rather quickly to quite flat. In post-liberation years, in our school days, we used to often listen to those exciting stories from our school teachers in classrooms as vivid depiction of their pseudo-war experience, probably quite fresh in their memories then. A lot of ungrateful people instead of paying tributes to Indian Air Force's contributions in the War of Liberations, often used to blame the aerial bombings as needless redundant like Hiroshima and Nagasaki and viewed them as deliberate acts to destroy Ayub-made infrastructure. Also, people used to complain alongside with most Urdu-speaking Pakistan Brutal Forces as POW, Indian Army also took away all leftover military hardware and industrial machineries *leaving only the cows behind*. These were all in post-BAKSAL period, was an interesting political phase as Zia was in charge. He floated his own political party in 1978, with support from a fraction of the population of Bengali-speaking Nationals of Pakistan (BNP). Fed up with No-Action-People (NAP) compared to Action-Loving (AL) people in other political stream, since the late 1960s, Bhasani had been in a "giveaway or sadaqah mode" for all his blessed political sons starting in 1969 Anti-Ayub Movement to the 1970s famous and decisive election under Yahya Khan regime in United Pakistan or many other diverse roles later in Bangladesh era. War ravaged, disillusioned societies in late 1970s had fresh and fond memories of the 1965 war when they were unscathed compared to the bloody and painful experience of Liberation War in 1971. Due to generic accusation culture, they had already started to put entire misfortune and blame of post-liberation time to India. A good percentage of the population secretly cherished there should be another referendum if people wanted to form a confederation with Pakistan under the six-point basis as they felt BD needed life support for its survival—either it had to integrate back to India or Pakistan. In fact, Zia and Bhasani never let it happen to put clock backward rather put few *Chapters in Sealed Classified Mode* and left them for time to move forward with. However, like he returned Dhanmondi 32 to current Bangladesh prime minister, Zia probably could have started the trials of killings of August 15, 1975, so that his widow and sons could never celebrate fake birthday on that day. In contrast to celebration modes of subcontinent people all over the world, including in the US on August 14 and 15, Bangladesh should continue to do soul searching, particularly on August 15, as for why they are quite different from the rest of the subcontinent people.

Coming back to school, except in very rare cases in the universities in advanced Western societies, you will never find universities recruiting their own PhD graduates as the faculties. In that view, the practice of recruiting in a faculty position just after four-year Master's degree in the same campus is a ridiculous practice being done all over Bangladesh. For university education, BD needs to follow Indian system as they have correctly maintained British heritages and have also integrated other major education traits of the world with demand of time. India does not let anyone take a faculty position just after a four-year degree.

Anyway, after defending my PhD thesis, I had to stay in Texas Tech University's Lubbock campus for quite a few reasons as Mehnaz Rinik, my daughter was born just a couple of months after my PhD defense. Also, I was putting some efforts in wrapping up the extension works beyond my PhD thesis and also virtually handling over my projects to the next graduate student in the lab. All the PhD committee members and faculties used to say to me, as I came across them quite often those days, "Now you need to move on and find your way out." That culture had not been quite uncommon as Americans have been quite good to drive away their own kids from their homes. For our Asian culture, it is painful though, as we expect free three meals a day and shelter from home *forever*. That time I was being interviewed for a post-doc position from two to three places and still I had my position in RU campus. Sayma had started her rehearsing of "complain culture"—that she gained nothing so far by living in the US—but was still reluctant to go back to BD's caverns. Instead of my original plan to go back to that secured bunker, I felt like I might continue to stay in insecure and uncertain ways and should start my refugee life. Being born in Rajshahi town, I had generic plantlike properties and liked to continue to stay in places for longer years. However, people in Texas Tech Campus and in the Physics Department started to ask, "Did you really graduate?" That was too much humiliation to me as a newly minted physics PhD. However, I knew showing them a diploma would lead to the next question, "Then why you are here?" Often, I use that very same tone to ask around some people I do like, "How come you are here?"

Journals of New York City || June 19, 2020
Oakland Gardens, New York

My Way Is the Highway and Refugee Routes, Roundabouts . . .

["Dedicated to the Nesting Dads and Moms of the World"]

When I left RU campus in beginning of 2001, I was almost getting close to complete my three-year term to file application to become an assistant professor. Although born in a family without any PhDs, our earning family members in fact used to make their living via publishing papers and working on patents in Rajshahi Science lab, in Bangladesh context, of course. During all my time in RU in BD, I never had any perception that academia meant publishing papers. It might be due to the fact that after Bangladesh became independent from Pakistan, most public universities got "Indemnity Ordinance" from such academic death penalty order, immunizing them from wrath of well-known "publish or perish" paradigm. So bottom line is, you could survive in the campus with all honors and dignities, even could get promoted to highest level without the trouble of getting involved in the publishing process at all. And I did embrace and love those ideas and rules and was 100 percent in compliance accordingly when I started my job in February 1998. Most young faculties in Applied Physics and Electronics Department during that time used to have antipathy to do research just to publish papers as they used to have unjustified poor respect for the articles that the senior faculties all over the campus were publishing. Overall, the trending philosophy was, "We are in unique RU campus and will continue to stay and grow and never would leave the boundaries of RU; then what is the need for so many papers? After all we are radio-mechanics and electronics troubleshooters and that we should and would focus more on that definition." In those days, to me private definition of science was "If your physics and electronics textbook's problem solutions and numbers match the textbook's answers, you get the highest achievements and joy of science," and that was absolutely in conformity with the "no-paper culture," except the fact you use pencil on paper for doing physics and electronics textbook problems.

I was planning to prepare my vitae for promotion to assistant professor and to include in that extra-curricular activities as I did win table-tennis (Ping-Pong) championship for both singles and doubles in the year 2000 in indoor games events of Applied Physics and Electronics Department. My next dream was to become runners-up in Ping-Pong doubles in RU teachers' club as we used to have a formidable duo in Ping-Pong doubles who individually used to be the champion and the runner-up in singles for many continuous years. And unless they retire or leave RU campus, it was simply impossible to beat them with my Ping-Pong skills learned and borrowed also from them. I thought that Ping-Pong efforts were important academic efforts then as my dad used to tell in his entire contract bridge career hardly he lost any game in his extra-curricular activities. In fact, he was common room contract bridge champion in the University of New South Wales for three consecutive years. As a prodigal son, I often used to tell Mom, "Maybe that's why dad never had a PhD." My mom was in contrast to my wife Sayma and had great respect for my dad's intellectual ability like that generation of all great moms. My mom gave me the impression, "Intellectually, contract bridge had been a lot more challenging than PhDs. Because many of dad's opponents in Dacca club, RawalPindi, and Sydney used to have PhDs." When dad discovered that I got prematurely addicted to smoking and auction bridge card games during my school days, he offered to teach me contract bridge to perhaps have a close watch over me. However, I used to avoid direct learning from my dad as a common practice in our generation is a Mom used to be closer than dad in family communications." Some exceptions perhaps here but some key philosophies in life that have both failing and passing aspects are, however, all borrowed from my dad. And in most cases, I did pursue my own whims perhaps always in the line of "My way is the highway . . ."

Endnote: Unfortunately, I left RU campus a little before all my colleagues and friends had started to come back from abroad with their PhDs. I lost some golden opportunities to learn about new knowledge and doctrines from their experience that I so badly in need of even today. Also, when I left RU campus, I did not realize it would take fourteen more years in 2015 just to become an assistant professor that was in fact originally due in 2001. Even after that, after continuous four years in there, I found other pathways to go back to original family profession of "only research and no teaching." So I have been on same refugee track as before, just on a different path perhaps . . .

Journals of New York City// June 21, 2020
Oakland Gardens, New York City

EPISODE # 9

Science Fair and PowerPoint Science

Kids do have tremendous curiosity. Until they reach their teenage years perhaps they do learn so rapidly from so many sources, including asking parents a lot of questions. However, when they become teenagers, they realize parents' knowledge and wisdom are kind of lagging and stereotyped, and actually do not match their newly achieved creativity and knowledge gathered via Instagram, Snapchat through the silicon network. Of course, schools do also play roles over seemingly drawn-out previous oldie sources of info. The teens reach the first of their knowledge-induced "don't care peak" due mainly to freshly acquired invincible info. I see the other side of this aspect of "Teenage Crisis" from some funny observations way back a few years ago when my daughter was not in her teens. I used to set aside a couple of days in a year to volunteer judging science projects for K-12 students. In those particular days, I had to drop Sayma to Bombay Theater in Queen's Fresh Meadows areas for "Maashla cum MaashAllah Movie" as she found that my "No-purpose Science Volunteer Judge" choice was "simply a waste of time for priceless weekends." My daughter was then too young to have her own opinion then and naturally used to stay with mom and that stance has not changed much, except for a teen's poor opinion about "Maashla cum MaashAllah Movie" with time later on. However, for some reasons, if not a Hindi movie connoisseur, I have been a great fan of Hindi/Urdu songs myself for music and tone. And I used to rely on Sayma for lyrics translation as she used to communicate meanings and simultaneously pointed out how remote and almost opposite my stand had been compared to that lyrics of actor's words/commitments to actress' soul and mind in that duet ☺:)

Going back to science events, I did notice an interesting pattern that I'd like to share with you all here, guessing you may or may not agree. When you ask questions to participants to assess the projects for prize considerations via grading, the participants from elementary to middle grades seemed truly passionate in terms of their genuine scientific curiosity about the project. Students in those categories seemed to have a lot of enthusiasm about their projects and were telling scientific stories with such interest and zeal that I used to feel ashamed of myself if I ever did have such interest in science myself anytime. But when you question the high school participants, most participants were more focused on presenting information in well-rehearsed words and manners than their own words like elementary and middle grades. It seemed like they were dwelling more with worries related to prizes like grades in exams. These high school kids often make smooth transition to Prezi and PowerPoint worlds and reach peak in their career like happy butterflies. If you bother to stop him or her by your testing questions, they never do feel ashamed to say "I don't know" and will move on to the next comfortable place/person going forward. When I hear about a lot of students in BD, after their SSC and HSC results are out, committing suicide, I do truly feel sad for them compared to such comfortable pattern for same age group in other parts of the world. Because in Western practice, if a student receives an A in exam they say, "I got an A" and if they receive a C, then they say, "The instructor gave me a C." So the kids in BD should be counseled before they sit for exams, not to take the entire responsibility of outcome of exam results in that extreme way particularly for an ill-designed SSC and HSC curriculum. In global context, BD's SSC and HSC systems had been truly shabby through all the years ever since BD became independent. Due to socio-economic reasons, the workforce involved in teaching, designing, and grading SSC and HSC exams had been less privileged in society, which is pity, compared to many other professions as most of them had been forced to take their jobs and reluctantly deliver that with zero and negative incentives. Of course, this underprivileged statement is not intended to demean their immense fortune earned via private tutoring. Based on that economic security, they were often engaged in spreading fears and bleak outcomes of failure/ poor performance in SSC/HSC exams and subsequent projected picture among their students. As most folks involved in that enterprise were miserable for most students, except for a few handful disciples of their choice. Motivating an entire class of students to meaningful career destinations had been a too far-fetched expectation. Only if they could just play an active role in stopping suicide of kids working along with parents would be a great effort from all sides. As currently perhaps many of them are just focused to work with small group of disciples or private students for tutoring, included in that group are a couple of other unavoidable vocal-performing students—and all in very dubious education scheme. All these SSC/HSC activities based on meaningless curriculum had really does not have much relevant roles in stimulating individual thinking so badly needed in the next level of university education. Prolonged practices of such culture at root education level over the decades have resulted in very chaotic academic muddled water in BD that people with little better academic credentials or political influence can easily fish on happily forever, particularly if you have a PhD degree from abroad. Unfortunately, the legacy of "Pondit Moshai" by timeless Syed Mujtaba Ali seems to be still working in some form or other with severe negative outcomes of persistence nature of chronic intellectual disease syndrome in the society.

Going back to COVID-19 days, in the very first known knowledge competition, humans won the trophy and compliments from the majority angels. Interestingly, Eve was absent in that decisive competition and that event was never repeated again. As we find two opinions of angels as majority were clueless and submissive and the only single was haughty and arrogant. Humans as blessed species won the trophy and did secure initial "worry-less" position to live as a happy pair—until Satanic intervention, of course. Ironically, those events also show formation and presence of humans could transform an angel through Satanic form as well. With such initial stigma, let us hope as a species we have not been decreed to be wiped out from the earth quite soon for visible and invisible reasons. As you might remember, angels did not endorse the idea that we came into shape and form and in fact did object our formation in the very beginning; so you never know what is coming next. Good-hearted people with sound knowledge of the scripture can perhaps tell a bit more about hope here and what are in store for us in the coming days. Amen.

Journals of New York City || June 28, 2020
Oakland Gardens, New York

EXIT # 10 \<Service Area Ahead\> GIGO Science and UNC Nobel Laureates

My two years in Wichita, Kansas, since January 2001 was drawing to a close. After fortunately getting a research assistantship from Texas Tech University in the following year of spring 2002, I was heavily overwhelmed by self-complacencies and, hence, losing friends in the Wichita area. One nano-tech professor from Texas Tech University (TTU) called me via phone to join the industry-funded semiconductor lab as a PhD student in TTU campus immediately. For some reason, the professor was liking the legacies of "Tetris games in our Thin Solid Films Lab" back in Rajshahi University in Bangladesh days and was asking bit details of that work as it had been on my transcripts along with several communication engineering courses used to be taught therein. Seeing a strong resemblance of my electronics and applied physics background with electrical engineering (EE), the professor offered me to transfer to EE PhD program. I was gently declining and telling the professor, "Rain or shine, I want my PhD in physics . . . Period." Looking back, it might have been a poor decision in terms of job markets/job prospects as EE PhDs no doubt make more money than many other professions. When I told my wife Sayma of that phone conversations later (she was not with me in Wichita that time), she considered I just wasted my best opportunity in life through my indiscretion and asked me, "If you go back in time, what would you have done?" Obviously you cannot expect for people in BD origin to put physics ahead of electrical or any other engineering, in most cases. So my answer surprised her totally as I told her, "I will do the same mistake again, again and once again." Is that the definition of insanity? "doing the same mistake again and again"? Thank God we do not go back in time to correct or keep wrong decisions, anyway. That means physics PhDs are actually quite sane, folks, and they just might have or have not done one mistake in their academic life.

Coming back to Wichita State University campus, perhaps I was the only and the last graduate student who used "transparencies" to defend an MS thesis instead of PowerPoint. My antipathy to adopt state-of-art tools was nothing new here. As you all remember how Windows 95 in 1995–96 took over the world. Many new computer users were just became very efficient IT experts in that 1995–2000 period. Also, like the COVID-19 virus now, there used to be a fear of virus called Millennium virus/bug that was about to sweep the world and all the computers and IT backbones—it never happened that way though. Despite all my friends and seniors' advice in 1996–97 to switch to MS Word and MS Excel, I avoided using mouse and decided to type the thesis in DOS-based WordPerfect and all the plots in Harvard Graphics programs. I thought I could continue to use computer using DOS mode and persistently was not interested to make transition to new trends in mouse and GUIs in Windows 95. Ordinary people like me cannot create their own course against the stream of time. But I have seen people up close, who have since the 1960s, never changed programming languages other than ForTran and still solving many complex scientific problems with that single classic tool. By the way, Intel company still makes very updated ForTran compiler as a lot of well-tested codes from the past are still good as gold than many kids' apps in smartphones nowadays. Those people hardly use other people's software license or utility tools to generate GIGO to publish numerous papers and count secretly who are citing their works and posting/boasting with set of *non-sense statistics*. Rather these people have been hardcore developers themselves, can troubleshoot, design algorithm, and implement software and not like the majority of GUI or Google-button people. Running codes by himself or depending on someone else even for that trivial part, collecting numbers and populating tables, and making some plots thereof and then looking for reports from workers from the Western world to feel safe and complacent, followed by a few pages of writing to defend those numbers and plots are the definition of intellect here, maybe for many of us. How can you expect people to assess you differently from such plague and shower you laurels after laurels?

Luckily, most people do not have or carry such feelings to earn laurels for themselves. When I was a post-doc in UNC Chapel Hill in 2007–08, for the first time in the history of UNC, a currently affiliated Professor Oliver Smithies (deceased) won the Nobel Prize in Physiology and Medicine. All the graduate students, post-docs, faculties, university staffs of UNC were truly in a celebratory mood as pizzas, donuts, alcoholic, and nonalcoholic drinks were all over the campus. I hope someday InshaAllah when Professor Zahid Hassan of Princeton University gets the Nobel Prize in Physics that we will all celebrate in strict halal/shariah way here.

Back in the UNC campus, we heard there was one aged professor who was not coming out from his office since Nobel news had been released in UNC channel in the morning and reported to be drinking heavily all alone by himself feeling badly depressed in self-quarantined mode, and not allowing anyone coming close to him. People acquainted with him said that the professor first thought the news from university sources was a hoax, and when he verified with national/international news sources, he became deeply frustrated and hopeless as he used to think himself to be the best scientist and professor in the UNC Chapel Hill campus. It was told he never expected someone could stole the march from him that way. Later, we heard a lot of people were leaving his lab as his dealings with his lab members were deteriorating day by day after the UNC Nobel Prize incidence. Anyway, my only winter in North Carolina was mild and nice as I moved to New York City in late September 2008 to have any meaningful follow-up on that story from some other lab folks, of course.

PS: A few years back, I heard that the professor in UNC Chapel Hill became quite a normal and nice person once again after another scientist from UNC Chapel Hill, Professor Aziz Sancar, won the Nobel Prize in Chemistry in 2015. Incidentally, our lipid fusion kinetics lab in now abandoned Mary Ellen Jones building in UNC Chapel Hill used to be on the same floor as the labs of Professor Aziz Sancar and his spouse, also a professor, Gwan Sancar. Both were very amicable and approachable persons and were willing to help post-docs and graduate students during that time. So far, that had been my closest interactions ☺:) with members of a Nobel Prize-winning family. However, Happy Fourth of July to all and I hope some remote Nobel Prize or Field medal does not destroy our peace here like what happened to that UNC Chapel Hill's professor in October of 2007. May God Bless America. Amen.

July 04, 2020
Journals of New York City
Oakland Gardens, New York

E P I S O D E   #   11

Nepotism, Academic Career, Human Fallacy

The human species on earth is going thru an interesting and uncertain period. Few months back in extreme locked-down phase we saw lot of interesting feature. One such feature was numerous monkeys were dancing in the streets of Manhattan. Monkeys must have been relishing complete absence of humans and were prevailing supreme all over the nooks and corners of Manhattan blocks even in some high-end neighborhoods. Prior to start of agriculture era, humans had quite vulnerable phases in jungles and wilderness fighting directly with other species for survival. With a culture of science and technology which other species does not apply or apparently not capable of applying at least collectively as culture and communication methods; human as a race has been successful in mitigating vulnerability from other visible species and in doing so they have already done substantial damages to the environments not only for themselves as a race rather for other species in the planet as well. However, most scriptures have given human sheer authority over other species in such actions. Although now-a-days lot of animal protection groups often make hot agenda with *animal distress* but the fact is nobody so far ever tries to establish a sovereign Cow-Land except for dairy farm purposes and interests I guess. So human adventure with his own culture of civilization so far has been growing with "obvious limited understandings of nature" and to apply it in lab or limited outdoor scale to get some tasks done in today's technology-based society. Looking back in today's age of Airbus380, TomTom GPS, iPhone, Android and high speed supercomputers are in fact products of long term culture that started with industrial revolution in Europe. Before industrial revolution in Europe, Arab world was the center of science, arts and technology.

With madrasha-based education for quite a significant percentage of population, BD population in general has very poor perception to that rich heritage and history about center of civilization in middle age located in Arab peninsula. Instead of connecting with that rich culture, history as lawful successor to that heritage available to them proactively and use that resources to improve himself, culture, literature and surrounding communities as well; often they react and waste valuable energy in un-proportionate amount to reactionary and ill-motivated blogger type people and most cases loose that social battle and fall behind as economically dis-advantaged group. Like perhaps the world as now seeing clashes of civilizations between English and Mandranin Chinses speaking people. In past there used to be glorious conflicts between Roman and Arab civilizations. It is unfortunate even after doing all the ground works that were needed for a full-fledged mechanized industrial revolutions, industrial revolution actually did happen in Europe and not in the Arab world. Besides mechanized industrial revolution all the mind boggling theories of 20th century physics that actually have given human precision understanding of the nature than traditional civil, mechanical or other engineering can offer to teach here actually originated in European universities or even in patent office localized in Europe. In past I lost friendship with one of my closest friends of engineering origin to define "civil engineering as mere an empirical science". However, a group of people via only that skills have accumulated massive amount of fortune in BD also in elsewhere and are still thriving in corruption. Coming back to the exodus of scientists from Europe in mass to USA has definitely changed shape of US science and technological land-scape over many other countries including former Soviet Union. Besides US born scientists, migrated scientists from Europe was a vital factor for phenomenal growth of US science and technology in post second world war and COLD WAR period of course. Apparently Europe never ran short in talents even after so many that fled the continent and still Europe is the center of many scientific fields including high energy particle physics of course.

When I came to New York City first, I realized I was an outsider with my American credentials in this great city. The academia in New York City and Boston areas are more connected across the Atlantic and hence with Europe than across Continent to southern or mid-west part of the USA. In fact, New York City welcomes Europe-trained manpower more than any other places in USA. Initially I was so upset with these facts when I moved here; that in one job interview I was literally yelling to the search chair to look and consider my US-based physics PhD quall exam and subject test scores before asking upsetting physics basic questions to ridicule a candidate for his basics ☺:) Seemingly search chair was giving air he was in substitute role after demise of great Lev Landau. However, the rest search committee members were mixed in dealings and let me cool off bit after such exasperation and in fact did ask many sensible nice even sometimes not so nice personal questions like US immigration status, how big is the family etc. etc. ☺:) . When I told Sayma of that interview outcome she heaved a great sigh and gave thanks to God that at least it did not happen in BD as you can tell outcomes here for such academic outburst to a god-father controlled job boards in BD campuses.

One last thing I really did not want to mention here as I feel RU gave me lot in past than I really did deserve. But I need to mention it here just for tallying for tallying's sake. In West, if you have a family member or relative in an institution where you are applying for a job you need to mention that in your application explicitly. Of course your relative can not and should not influence your selection for any competitive processes like exam scores both theory and experiment, jobs, scholarships, promotions etc. and also should not send recommendation letters for you in general for such case. If you achieve something not strictly following those basic norms that this certainly a stigma on you and on your career and gross misconduct in your life and academic career. Instead of interpreting via sharia/halal mashala or as might/rights of minorities you better should spend time on self-reflection on your sordid secret/open academic gains. But do not forget that we all are humans and can do mistakes in life. And future good works can certainly obliterate all past shortcomings here for sure. May God show us the right path here. Amen.

Journals of New York City || July 10, 2020
Oakland Gardens, New York

EPISODE # 12

Bill Gates and Scientists

In USA or in general in academia of North America two universities from Bangladesh are well known; BUET and DU. RU probably never been in harmony with US academics since they vandalized the USIS office in the 1970s. Yes, there used to an USIS in present Kandahar of BD :) So the point here, does not matter how red your soul and mind have been all through your life; your physical nourishments had been from the wheat of PL-480; before booming of BD-based garment industries you did learn about Used Wools and T-shirts from "Nixon market" of Sahib Bazar, although many moms that generation never used that stuff due to traditional prejudices even in extreme economic hardship of 1970s. However, I found nothing unscientific in other popular choice there after adequate disinfection practices like Covid cautions; but lab science does not control your home practice behavior always. Like that contradictory facts that you had been a staunch supporter of former Soviet-India axis, used to protest against wherever 7th fleet used to roam around but now you feel yourself lucky that you are part of this blessed land, USA.

Although you never feel rapport with general people of Pakistan obviously for low per capita income but you have been with people of USA ever since your life even with your broken English to ameliorate your extreme commitments to memories of former Soviet-India allegiances and "Down with Imperialism" slogan. It can happen and nothing unusual as lot of Bengali speaking people used to support Pakistan or India during cricket matches as late as 2000 by choice but still being part of Independent Bangladesh. Personally I had been brought up to believe all things Arabs did to Israel had been halal when in BD, but working in Mount Sinai for long years I learned another term called Kosher which is like the other side of same coin. However, trinity makes me nervous as that totally contradicts monotheism (God forbids) and absolutely neither halal nor kosher. Probably era of Ottoman Empire teaches better here as Erdogan doing lot better jobs now probably than Kazi Nazrul could think of Komol (soft) Ata :) Still, whenever possible, majority should entertain sentiment of minorities and reassure them with good gesture and heart instead of finding flaws in their hidden minds and actions. As everyone has comfort zones, beliefs, sentiments and you cannot force him/her to your sole brand of halal/shariah route. Like in BD universities, PhDs from Harvard/MIT/Stanford/Caltech or Oxford/Cambridge/ANU are quite few and rare and should be treated with appropriate honors with respects as deserved.

Western societies have different outlook here as it correctly recognize iconic Bill Gates and in past Steve Jobs as well and endorse them not wasting too much time in formal campus education. Personally I am of opinion people like Gates or Jobs did lot more to human race and to the planet than many regular Nobel Laureates. If you attend scientific conferences regularly and talk with reasonable people at frontiers not like many other irrational dis-grunted professors you will recognize one fact, not always those frontier people have been happy with 2/3 people being selected in month of October each year to alter history and facets of science culture for future generations. Few examples you may agree or may not agree: [Case A] Freeman Dyson was left out from quantum electrodynamics field theory winners way back quite a time ago. Interestingly Dyson never had a PhD. So you really do not need a PhD or academic degree to do real scientific good works! Only problem most people are not like Dyson and can be filtered out easily by that PhD sieve to have severe obstacles placed in front to prove by his/her rest life that s/he is better than Dyson :) [Case B] Ali Javan was cut out from laser winners. It is not that being myself an *Ali* here in a spectators' gallery and due to that I have bias in opinion for another *Ali*. But if you look through carefully you will agree Trump-like people have been in existence and plenty in numbers in all areas including in science for decades :) [Case C] This is recent and really disturbing and happened in a field called GPCR type protein. GPCR is a kind of transducer protein that communicates with cell's interior with cell's exterior and has been very elusive cell membrane protein to learn about as almost 50% of marketed drugs target that protein and brings effects like "homeopathy" :) for our well-fare.

The person who first solved the structure like Watson-Crick did for DNA or Pauling for alpha-helix of protein was Krzysztof Palczewski. Unfortunately he was left out from the list in 2012. This list can be really long and big here. Whatever, interestingly those people never left science or quit their works from rejection/selection :) Probably that makes scientists which we have never been any closer by any standard for sure! So stay relaxed and enjoy your weekend bro :)

PS/ Please overlook miss-spelt words as I do not feel like checking spellings here :) As no fear are there to loose points as we used to have during SSC/HSC years :)

Friday Evening, July 17, 2020
Oakland Gardens, New York
Journals of New York City

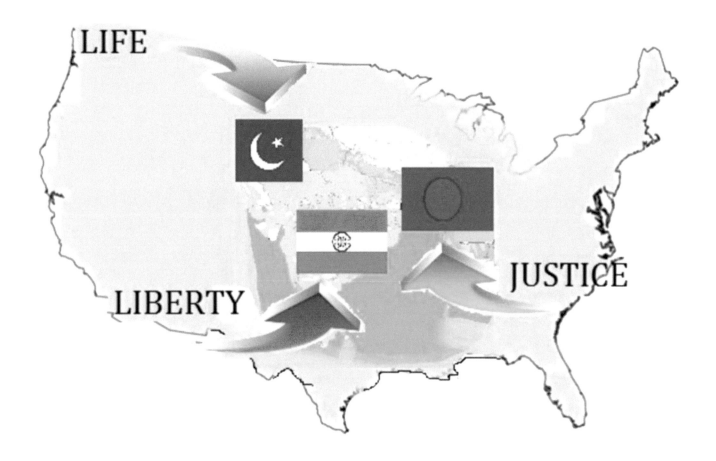

LIFE

LIBERTY

JUSTICE

Episode # 13

August 14 and 15

When in summer of 2004 we came to visit New York City for the 1st time just for 7/10 days driving over 1500 miles all way from Lubbock, Texas with another student family, we never thought NYC would be the future abode for now almost 12 years. University of Alabama at Birmingham had always showed me ample generosity of south with welcoming gesture that I did decline on two different occasions for independent post-doc positions. However, the decision to move into NYC from North Carolina was not that easy. Due to proximity of my work place in today's Tandon School of Engineering of NYU and Sayma's CUNY's Brooklyn campus we found an apartment close by Brighton line of NYC's subway system in Midwood region of Brooklyn. Even though it was not Jackson Heights in Queens Borough but still a nice Bangla pocket in Brooklyn, King's County of NYC☺. Lot people claimed immigrants from Bangladesh in New York City first settled in that part in Brooklyn compared to widely held view that they first came and settled in Jackson Heights. Our daughter Mehnaz Rinik picked up a strange Bangla dialect mainly from her baby sitter of Bangladesh origin in same apartment complex. Although Sayma listens and likes Rabindra songs and big fan of them but my bad influence made her listen to that type of music less and less and at low audible volume. Well Rabindra sangeet after all not like 7th March speech so low volume is quite reasonable there I guess compared to unique voice of Mujib in 1971. So deviation from puritan view made us less reactive to Mehnaz Rinik's funny Bangla talk as many cultured people would have fainted listening to such distorted version of standard Bangla. Due further to my bad influence, Mehnaz Rinik started to like Humayun's "Maro Chika" song from "Package Songbad" and gets quickly into party mood and we all love that as true Bangla culture, Alhamdulillah ☺One further thing, NYC publishes countless number of Bangla Newspapers and NYC edition of some Dhaka-based Bangladesh dailies as well. As you will find ubiquitous presence of Bangla all over the NYC and that feature is growing more and more as Bangla is well-known as one of major languages spoken in NYC. Interestingly it seems "Maro Chika" type version of Bangla is getting popular over standard and cultured Bangla in an irreversible and definitive ways all over the NYC. Maybe London or Toronto can be centers of pure Bangla in future who knows. However, with more people from Sylhet/Noakhali regions particularly in London compared to Toronto or NYC, recovering Bangla in original pure form will be a lost hope as the general trends are showing so far. But since language is a dynamic feature in human culture and intellect developments, some experiments in limited scale can always be done in very halal/shariah ways, InshaAllah.

Going back to Texas Tech University campus in summer 2004, as I was starting research after the PhD qual and my advisor was mentoring me in fluorescence microscopy and spectroscopy, enzyme kinetics in experiments as well as in lattice Monte Carlo technique in computational biophysics. In US campuses when you pass the PhD qual exam you start to get kind of "Jamai" (Bangla word for son-in-law) like treatment from the departmental faculties. Of course, that does not mean faculties do carry hidden agenda there to let their daughters or nieces to date with you and eventually get married like that often used to happen in RU campuses ☺Rather they felt like these folks had gone past the "Curses of Goldstein and Jackson" (see note below) and literate enough to talk seriously and worth to share quality time with in the faculty offices and occasionally in the restaurant, coffee houses in off-campus locations. Also the facts have been most PhD students were married or at least living with partners in US social context by the time they made thru qual exams. During those years, I had added advantages as my advisor just received a big NSF grant that meant I could focus all my time to research and taking few more required courses and no extra work as Teaching Assistant. During my transition from device physics to biophysics in period 2003-2004; I was assigned as Teaching Assistant (TA) as my original device physics group where I was (Research Assistant) RA than TA, left TTU for Mizzou (University of Missouri at Columbia) in summer 2003. I opted to stay in TTU rather moving to Mizzou's physics program. Anyway during all my PhD years, my PhD advisor never objected and did always allow my wife Sayma to accompany in conferences all over USA as we together partitioned time between Science and Sight-Seeing ☺Departmental Head Professor Lynn Hatfield (deceased) was generous gentle man and used to support at least one conference in a year from departmental resources. So it was additional Science with Sight-Seeing option not uncommon as graduate student.

But post-doc times are different as you need to learn swimming in ocean besides learning bike riding perhaps. If your head is too heavy compared to your light-gravity body then obviously you going to drown down here in academic sea-bed. I painfully realized Europeans have reasons to feel proud of their training compared to my complacency in passing physics PhD qual on first effort in a medium-level US university! Anyway my legacy of Rajshahi Science lab did help here as perseverance is the best way for a top-to-bottom stupid student to keep afloat and survive! In one and half year, I did solve what I expect to do as post-doc research problem. Making molecular dynamics movies for the lab became my passion as my post-doc mentors started to call me "the Movie Director" in the group meetings. Some of the animation movies are still playing in YouTube. The fact I was getting paid $10K/year less than my very first job in New York City hardly did bother me as science in Mount Sinai has been truly exciting! Lot of my Facebook scientist friends may or may not agree when something works in science is the best joy than just getting a paper accepted in a journal. So instead of being too critical of Dr. Zafar Iqbal or Professor Jamal Nazrul Islam (deceased) for their personal life styles and choices; one should respect the facts that they made some projects working in challenging scientific environments. After all AT&T Bell Lab never did hire that dumb people likewise Cambridge University Press usually does not publish crappy type text books ☺

Anyway after few days of living in Midwood part of Brooklyn, I realized that part of New York City had been more of Mini-Pakistan than Mini-Bangladesh. Just couple of blocks from our apartment place contrast to 1200 miles before/after 1971, we used to have Coney Island Avenue and that has been truly the hub of Pakistan in New York City. Sayma's fluency in Hindi/Urdu made shopping in India/Pakistan pockets in New York City and New Jersey areas highly discounted and pleasant experience as I never have hidden my political opinion of splitting sub-continent into India/Pakistan/Bangladesh as true unfortunate events that could happen in history. Partitioning in 1947 laid foundation of intolerance, violence and escalation of tension, mistrust among communities and insecurity in societies. In its undivided form with tremendous diversity of culture and religions, India had the potential to become next United States of the world starting in 1947. However, with current type of prime minister in New Delhi that thinking of tolerance, secularism and human rights of minorities will be just far-fetched here. However, Pronob Mukherjee has been probably bit different here and India needs more leaders like him and we hope he gets well soon. In my opinion sub-continent has many Jinnahs or Nehruhs but very few Gandhis, Maolana Azads and Bongobondhus. So August 14 and 15 are important dates in sub-continent for reflections and we wish prosperity of all people as we carry same history and heritage under British rule for almost 200 years!

PS/ Goldstein (Classical Mechanics) and Jackson (Electrodynamics) are used here as the texts in most US physics programs. The books are famous among experts and infamous for struggling graduate students.

Journals of New York City
Oakland Gardens, New York
August 14, 2020

Printed in the United States
By Bookmasters